Barack O

Saddleback's Graphic Biographies

SADDLEBACK
EDUCATIONAL PUBLISHING
www.sdlback.com

ISBN-13: 978-1-59905-453-7
ISBN-10: 1-59905-453-1
eBook: 978-1-60291-779-8

Printed in Guangzhou, China
0411/04-21-11

15 14 13 12 11   2 3 4 5 6 7 8

Before Barack Obama was president, he lived in many different places and met many different kinds of people. Growing up, Barack had to work hard to understand himself and the world around him.

A few months after his twenty-first birthday, the future president found out his father had died in a car accident. He had only met his father once, when he was ten years old.

At the 2004 Democratic National Convention in Boston, Massachusetts, Illinois State Senator Barack Obama gave the keynote address.

Barack told different stories about his father in Honolulu, Hawaii, in December 1971.

My grandfather, see, he's a chief.
It's sort of like the king of the tribe.
So that makes my father a prince. He'll
take over when my grandfather dies.

None of the stories
Barack told his
classmates were true.
Barack's grandfather,
Onyango Obama, was
a farmer and a cook.

What about after
that? I mean, will
you go back and
be a prince?

Well, if I
want to
I could.

But to be fair, when Barack was ten and everyone called him Barry, he didn't
know much about his father's family, or even the country that they came from.

Barrack's father, Barack Obama
Sr., was born in Kenya. He did well
in school and was invited to study
in the United States.

While he was at the University of
Hawaii, he met Barack's mother, Ann.

Ann Dunham met Barack Sr.
in a Russian language class.
They were married
February 2, 1961. In 1961
interracial marriage was
rare. Barack Sr.'s
father and Ann's parents
were not happy
with their children.

When Barack was two years old, his father finished studying at the University of Hawaii. Barack Sr. received two offers to continue his studies: One came from the New School in New York City, the other from Harvard University, in Cambridge, Massachusetts.

Why do you have to go to Harvard? If you choose New York, you'll have enough money to take us with you!

LOGIC

How can I refuse the best school?

Barack's parents split up soon after his father left for Massachusetts.

All Barack knew of his father came from the stories his mother and grandparents told him.

It's a fact Barry. Your dad could handle just about any situation.

Toot, remember the time he had to sing at that music festival? He'd agreed to sing some African songs.

But your dad sang by himself in front of this big crowd anyway.

And he wasn't great.

But it turned out be some big to-do, with professional bands?

Yep!

Barack called his grandparents Gramps and Toot, which came from tutu, the Hawaiian word for "grandmother."

No, but he was so sure of himself that the crowd loved him. There's something you can learn from your dad. Confidence. The secret to success.

4

Barry, come here! I have someone I want you to meet. This is Lolo, Mommy's friend from the university.

Lolo Soetoro came from the country of Indonesia, and was in Hawaii studying geography.

Ann and Lolo married when Barack was six years old. Soon after, Lolo had to return home to Indonesia. Ann decided that she and Barack would join him.

Barack's grandparents responded to the news in their own ways.

I better pack you some more canned food.

Here we go. Indonesia. It's a chain of islands, like Hawaii. Says here they got tigers over there. And apes!

Ann and Barack moved to Indonesia a year after Lolo left Hawaii.

Lolo had changed during that year, starting with a new mustache.

Later, Ann would find out that Lolo was forced to return to Indonesia, to serve in the army.

Barack lived in Indonesia for four years, from ages six to ten. Life was different in Indonesia.

Barry ate things that most people in the United States do not eat.

He ate dog meat, snake meat, and roasted grasshopper; the meat was tough, the grasshopper crunchy.

It was also the first time Barack saw people living in terrible poverty.

In Indonesia, Barack and his mother saw poverty unlike anything they had experienced in the United States.

That is the Hotel Indonesia. Very modern. And Barry! Look!

That's Hanuman, the monkey god. He's a great warrior. Strong as a hundred men.

Ann would give Indonesian money, rupiah, to poor people whenever she could. Lolo encouraged Barack to keep his money for himself.

The house Lolo had bought for them in Jakarta, the capital city of Indonesia, was not very big. Lolo was working for the army, which didn't pay a lot.

Later, Lolo got a new job, working for an American oil company.

Hold on Barry. I have a surprise for you.

A monkey!

With the new job came a bigger house with a television, a radio, and servants.

An ape.

His name is Tata. I brought him all the way from New Guinea.

Don't worry. He's on a leash.

Oh. Good.

Barack had many difficulties. He not only had to learn a new language, he had to learn a new way of life, with different rules and values. Later, teachers would remember him as a quiet boy that sat in the back of the room, sometimes teased for being the only foreigner in the class.

At first, Ann wanted her son to get used to Indonesia.

...and my friend and I, we thought it would be fun to mudslide, and I didn't even see the barbed wire...

We have to get him to the hospital!

It's too late now. We can take him to get stitches in the morning.

Ann had a neighbor drive her and Barack to the hospital. There were only two doctors there. They would not give Barack stitches until they finished their game of dominoes.

More and more, Ann thought that America would be a better place for Barack.

Mom! I'm tired!

This is no picnic for me either, buster!

Ann began waking Barack up at 4 a.m. every day to teach him English before he went to school and she went to work.

And she would tell him that he got his intelligence from his father.

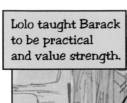 Lolo taught Barack to be practical and value strength.

Men take advantage of weakness in other men. They're just like countries in that way.

 The strong man takes the weak man's land. He makes the weak man work in the fields. Which would you rather be?

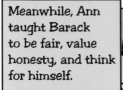 Meanwhile, Ann taught Barack to be fair, value honesty, and think for himself.

 If you want to grow into a human being, you're going to need some values!

In 1970, Ann gave birth to Maya Soetoro, Barack's half sister.

Lolo had not been talking to Ann much, but they seemed closer after Maya was born, at least for a while.

 When Barack was 10, he moved back to Hawaii to live with his grandparents. He started the fifth grade at a private school called the Punahou School. The school was expensive, but Barack got a scholarship.

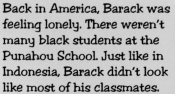

Back in America, Barack was feeling lonely. There weren't many black students at the Punahou School. Just like in Indonesia, Barack didn't look like most of his classmates.

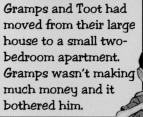

Gramps and Toot had moved from their large house to a small two-bedroom apartment. Gramps wasn't making much money and it bothered him.

Gramps and Toot fought more. They never took Barack to the beach as they had when he was younger.

It's a telegram from your mother. She's coming to visit for Christmas. And, Barry, it looks like your father is coming to visit too.

Should be one heck of a Christmas.

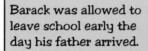

Barack was allowed to leave school early the day his father arrived.

Well, Barry. It is a good thing to see you after so long. Very good.

During the visit, Barack and his father didn't speak very much.

But Barack Sr. did talk at his son's school. Barack's teacher, Ms. Hefty, had once lived in Kenya, and invited Barack Sr. to come speak.

We have a special treat for you today. Barry Obama's father is here. He's come all the way from Kenya, in Africa, to tell us about his country.

You know, Kenya and America are not so different.

In both countries we struggled under the British, who tried to rule unjustly. Many in Kenya were made slaves because of the color of their skin, just like in America. And Kenyans, like all of you in this room, long to be free and become better people through hard work and sacrifice.

This is our house Barack, and it's almost Christmas vacation. If Barry wants to watch the Grinch, he can!

You spoil the boy. He should be working harder in school. Much harder!

In the time they spent together, Barack and his father stayed far apart.

Barack Sr. stayed in Hawaii for a month. He had remarried by then and had six more children.

When the month ended, all that remained for Barack were a few photos and the basketball his father had given him for Christmas.

Soon after, Ann separated from Lolo and moved back to Hawaii with Maya. Barack moved in to a small apartment with Ann and Maya while Ann went back to the University of Hawaii to earn a Master's degree. Being raised by a poor single mom, Barack felt even more out of place among the wealthy students at Punahou.

When Barack was 13, his mother decided to move back to Indonesia because she loved the country. Ann and Lolo remained separated, divorcing in 1980.

Ann wanted Barack to come with her and Maya, but Barack chose to stay. He went back to live with Gramps and Toot.

With his father's gift in hand, Barack taught himself to play basketball on a playground near his grandparents' apartment.

By the time he entered high school, Barack was good enough to play on the Punahou team.

On the basketball court, Barack found a new group of friends.

Coach, we're killing this team! Our second string should be playing more! It's only fair!

And, he started to show the makings of a future politician.

During high school, Barack's life started turning down the wrong path. He was spending more time partying with his friends, and his grades suffered.

Ann wrote to Barack from Indonesia, concerned about her son's future. She told him about the work she did helping poor people who didn't have the advantages he had in Hawaii. And she said he should go to college. Barack did as she said.

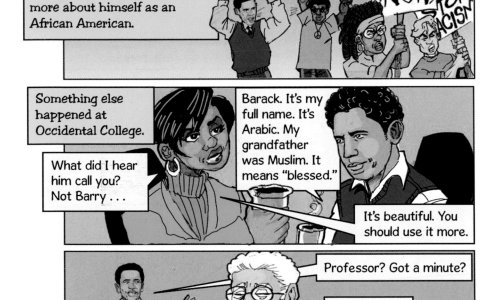

After high school, Barack won a scholarship to Occidental College. He also began to think more about himself as an African American.

STOP RACISM!

END APARTHEID

DIVEST NOW!

STOP RACISM

Something else happened at Occidental College.

What did I hear him call you? Not Barry . . .

Barack. It's my full name. It's Arabic. My grandfather was Muslim. It means "blessed."

It's beautiful. You should use it more.

Professor? Got a minute?

Sure Barack.

By the time he transferred to Columbia University Barack Obama was using the name his father gave him.

"That was all. The line cut off, and I sat down on the couch, smelling eggs burn in the kitchen, staring at cracks in the plaster, trying to measure my loss."

-from page 5 of Barack Obama's autobiography, *Dreams of My Father*.

Later that day, Barack called his mother to give her the news.
Ann cried on the phone. Barack didn't cry until a year later.

What was that all about?
Do you know your eggs
are burning?

In New York, Barack went to school, studied, and did little else. He didn't
talk to many people, and didn't have many close friends. To take breaks from
working, Barack would walk around the city.

All of Barack's hard work paid
off in 1983, when he graduated
from Columbia University with
a degree in political science.

After college, Barack
went to work as a
community organizer
in the poor black
neighborhoods on the
South Side of Chicago.
A community organizer
tries to get people to
work together to find
ways to improve
their neighborhood.

WELCOME TO
ALTGELD
HOUSING PROJECTS

Barack spent most of his time
working in Altgeld Gardens, a
poor housing project stuck in
between a factory, a landfill,
and the polluted Calumet River.

Barack tried to start working as an organizer by addressing big problems, like gangs or unemployment. However, not many people came to the meetings. Barack realized that, in order to get people to work together, he had to get to know the people first.

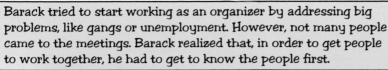

So, a lot of Barack's time was spent just listening to what people had to say about living in Chicago's housing projects.

That toilet's been backed up for months!

I told them that ceiling was going to fall in!

My son could break his neck, riding a bike in that broken street!

Mr. Obama, I saw this in the paper yesterday.

This says they're looking for someone to remove asbestos from the Altgeld management office!

Does that mean there is asbestos in our homes too?

Asbestos is a fireproof material. It was used in building houses until people found out that small bits of asbestos can make you very sick. The manager of Altgeld Gardens said that the houses had been tested for asbestos, but refused to show proof. So Barack and many people from the neighborhood rode in a bus to the Chicago Housing Authority, the government office supposed to take care of Altgeld.

Listen up everybody. We're going to go over what we'll say at this protest.

What do we want?

A meeting with the boss!

What if they say they'll give us an answer later?

We want an answer now!

The protest seemed to work. The director of the CHA promised to begin testing the houses for asbestos right way. The bus ride to the CHA office showed Barack the power of hope.

But some months later, the people from Altgeld Gardens were told there was enough money to remove the asbestos or fix leaking roofs, but not both. The people of Altgeld Gardens lost hope, and Barack decided he needed to go back to school.

After working in Chicago, Barack felt like he needed a law degree to truly help poor communities protect their rights. He was accepted into the law school at Harvard University in 1988. This was the same school his father went to after leaving him and his mother.

But then, Barack had already been following in his father's footsteps for several months.

Before starting school at Harvard, Barack spent five months in Kenya, visiting the places his father had called home. He met his father's family, including many of his own half-brothers and sisters. He also became very close with his father's stepmother, a woman he called Granny Sara.

Barack also visited his father's grave. Barack Sr. would have been proud to see what his son went on to do at Harvard.

At the end of his first year at Harvard, Barack was elected to be a law review editor. At the end of his second year, he became the first African American elected as president of the *Harvard Law Review*.

The historic moment was captured in an article in the *New York Times*. Soon after, Barack was commissioned to write what became his autobiography, *Dreams of My Father*. It was Barack's first experience with national attention.

In the summer between his first and second years at Harvard, Barack went to work for a big-money law firm in Chicago called Sidley & Austin. It was there that he met his wife.

Excuse me? Are you Michelle Robinson?

Yes?

Barack Obama. They said you'd tell me what I'd be working on.

. . . and that pretty much covers it. Any questions?

Just one. Where are you from?

South Side of Chicago.

No kidding! I used to do a lot of work down there.

Say, would you like to go out?

Sorry, I don't date co-workers.

Hey Michelle. Dinner ?

You sure don't give up. Not happening.

Take you out for coffee today?

Same answer as yesterday: No.

Buy you an ice cream cone?

Okay. Fine. An ice cream cone. But that's it.

Barack and Michelle were married in October 1992.

In 1994, Ann was diagnosed with cancer. Gramps had died two years earlier, so Ann moved back to Hawaii to be with Toot.

Soon afterwards, Barack began teaching constitutional law at the University of Chicago, a job he kept for 12 years.

Dr. Stanley Ann Dunham Soetoro passed away in 1995, at the age of 52.

Barack and Michelle's first daughter, Malia Ann Obama, was born three years later, in 1998.

Voters elected Barack to the Illinois Senate in November 1996. In 1997, he began representing the South Side of Chicago in the Old State Capitol building in Springfield, Illinois.

Later, in an interview, Barack's political director, Dan Shomon, described Barack's early political career.

It wasn't like Barack took Springfield by storm. The first few years he was thought of as intelligent, thoughtful, bright. But he certainly wasn't considered a major player.

When Dan Shomon began working for Barack, the two men drove up and down the state of Illinois to see how voters outside of Chicago would react to an African American senator.

There was still some racism in Southern Illinois.

We're just fact-finding. He's a state senator.

He's no state senator from these parts!

But overall, people in Illinois did not care about the color of Barack's skin.

That's funny! My grandfather used to say the same thing!

Barack decided to run for the United States Congress in the 2000 election. He began campaigning for a seat in the House of Representatives in 1999.

Barack was running against Representative Bobby Rush, who had held the seat for Illinois since 1993.

During the campaign, Barack and Michelle took Malia to Hawaii to see Toot. While they were there, Malia caught a bad cold.

Who called?

It was Dan. They need me back in Springfield to vote on the gun-control bill we supported. But I can't sacrifice Malia's health for politics.

The gun-control bill failed to pass in the Senate. The governor of Illinois was angry with Barack, and one of the biggest newspapers in the state criticized the senator.

We're only halfway through the campaign, and we've already lost the election.

Barack was right. He lost badly to Bobby Rush.

You seem like a nice young man, but Bobby just hasn't done anything wrong.

Barack returned to the Illinois Senate, determined to work harder for people in the state.

He became well known as a Democrat that worked with Republicans to find common ground and get laws passed.

And he kept thinking of running for the United States Congress.

In 2001, Michelle gave birth to the Obamas' second daughter, Natasha.

Hello little Sasha.

Barack decided it was important for him to run for the U.S. Senate in 2004. Soon after, John Kerry invited Barack to give the keynote address at the Democratic National Convention. Reporters followed Barack, Michelle, and their staff wherever they went. Barack became famous, recognized across the country.

If there's a child on the South Side of Chicago who can't read, that matters to me, even if it's not my child. If there's a senior citizen somewhere who can't pay for her prescription and has to choose between medicine and the rent, that makes my life poorer, even if it's not my grandmother.

If there's an Arab American family being rounded up without benefit of an attorney or due process, that threatens my civil liberties. It's that fundamental belief—I am my brother's keeper, I am my sister's keeper —that makes this country work. It's what allows us to pursue our individual dreams, yet still come together as a single American family.

He won the election for the United States Senate easily. He didn't stay there long.

After serving in the U.S. Senate for three years, on a freezing day in February 2007, Barack returned to the Illinois Old State Capitol. More than 15,000 people braved the winter weather to hear what he had to say.

I stand before you today to announce my candidacy for president of the United States!

Barack convinced Michelle to let him run for president by promising to quit smoking. He promised Malia and Sasha they would get a puppy once the election was over.

At the beginning of the primaries, Barack was up against eight other candidates. But, as the states voted, it came down to just two: Barack and Hillary Clinton. Hillary was the United States senator from New York, and a former first lady.

This election was historic.

During the election, Barack became one of the first politicians to successfully use the Internet to attract volunteers and voters.

I want you to say it with me: Yes we can!

YES WE CAN!

Barack worked to encourage the kind of hope he had seen during the bus ride to the CHA office in Chicago when he was a community organizer.

He also tried to keep his skin color from being an issue. But after Jeremiah Wright, the minister of the Obamas' Chicago church, made some angry comments about Hillary's campaign, Barack felt he had to respond.

As he had in times past, Barack called for cooperation. He expressed his belief that many different kinds of people could come together to build one America.

It requires all Americans to realize that your dreams do not have to come at the expense of my dreams; that investing in the health, welfare, and education of black and brown and white children will ultimately help all of America prosper.

Barack beat Hillary in the Democratic primary. He chose Senator Joe Biden to run for vice president.

They were running against John McCain, the U.S. Senator from Arizona, and Sarah Palin, the governor of Alaska.

Barack succeeded in convincing people that America needed fresh ideas in the White House.

Senator John McCain wants to continue the same failed policies we've had for the past eight years!

On October 20, Barack suspended his presidential campaign for a few days to spend time with Toot, who was very ill.

On November 2, Toot died from cancer, just two days before her grandson was elected president.

On November 4, 2008, 250,000 Obama supporters of all different colors and ages crowded together in Chicago's Grant Park to watch the election results.

At 11 p.m., Eastern Standard Time, the television networks announced that Barack Obama had won the election. Malia and Sasha were getting a puppy.

On January 20, 2009, in front of a crowd of over 1 million people, Barack Obama was sworn in as the 44th president of the United States, becoming the first African American president in the country's history.

In his first speech as president, Barack addressed the many challenges the country faced.

Today I say to you that the challenges we face are real, they are serious and they are many. They will not be met easily or in a short span of time. But know this America: They will be met.

As he had throughout his life, Barack expressed faith in the American dream: The idea that people can work together toward a common goal of freedom.

Saddleback's Graphic Fiction & Nonfiction

If you enjoyed this Graphic Biography ... you will also enjoy our other graphic titles including:

Graphic Classics

- Around the World in Eighty Days
- The Best of Poe
- Black Beauty
- The Call of the Wild
- A Christmas Carol
- A Connecticut Yankee in King Arthur's Court
- Dr. Jekyll and Mr. Hyde
- Dracula
- Frankenstein
- The Great Adventures of Sherlock Holmes
- Gulliver's Travels
- Huckleberry Finn
- The Hunchback of Notre Dame
- The Invisible Man
- Jane Eyre
- Journey to the Center of the Earth
- Kidnapped
- The Last of the Mohicans
- The Man in the Iron Mask
- Moby Dick
- The Mutiny On Board H.M.S. Bounty
- The Mysterious Island
- The Prince and the Pauper
- The Red Badge of Courage
- The Scarlet Letter
- The Swiss Family Robinson
- A Tale of Two Cities
- The Three Musketeers
- The Time Machine
- Tom Sawyer
- Treasure Island
- 20,000 Leagues Under the Sea
- The War of the Worlds

Graphic Shakespeare

- As You Like It
- Hamlet
- Julius Caesar
- King Lear
- Macbeth
- The Merchant of Venice
- A Midsummer Night's Dream
- Othello
- Romeo and Juliet
- The Taming of the Shrew
- The Tempest
- Twelfth Night

SADDLEBACK
EDUCATIONAL PUBLISHING